BIRDS

Nicola Davies

KINGFISHER

Contents

What is a bird?

Birds are everywhere! You can see them in forests, deserts, seas and cities. There are nearly 10,000 different kinds, but every one has wings, a beak, feathers and feet.

Feathers

Birds are the only animals to have feathers. Tail and wing feathers are stiff and strong, while body feathers are silky and soft.

Feet

All birds have scaly feet. They have four toes, for perching or grabbing prey. Eagles have strong talons on their toes.

Wings

Birds need wings and strong feathers to fly. The bald eagle has large, powerful wings which let it soar and dive fast to catch its prey.

Beak

Birds do not have teeth to bite or chew. They have beaks instead, to grab food whole or to peck it into bits. Every bird has the right shaped beak for the kind of food it eats.

Flying made easy

Birds are good at flying because their bodies are made for it. Their bones are hollow and light, and they have big muscles to beat their wings up and down.

Light as a feather

A bird's skeleton weighs less than all its feathers, so it can fly easily.

Safety first

These guillemots have found a safe place to nest high on a clifftop. Flying means they can reach such places, while their predators cannot.

Long-distance flights

The Arctic tern is the champion long-distance flyer. It flies 40,000 kilometres every year looking for food and places to nest.

Fast food

There are so many more places to eat when you can fly... grab a fruit from a treetop, pick some fish from the sea, or snatch a juicy insect right out of the air, as this bee-eater has done.

Ways of flying

Every kind of bird has a different way of flying, so they all have different shaped wings. Short wings are good for fast flapping and long wings help with gliding.

Up, up...

Taking off is very hard work! This dove has to jump up from the ground or from a perch, then start flapping hard to get higher and faster.

...and away!

As the dove moves forwards, the air rushing under its wings helps to hold it up, so it does not have to flap as hard.

n a flap

Hummingbirds have
short wings that can
flap very fast, so they
can hover in the air.

Hanging around

Vultures have long, broad
wings that catch the air,
so they can glide all day
and hardly flap at all.

Birds on the ground

Not all birds can fly. Some are too big, some use their wings for swimming instead and some can find food and safety without flying.

Big bird

An ostrich can weigh more than a person. It is too heavy to fly but it can run away from danger at speeds of 72 kilometres an hour.

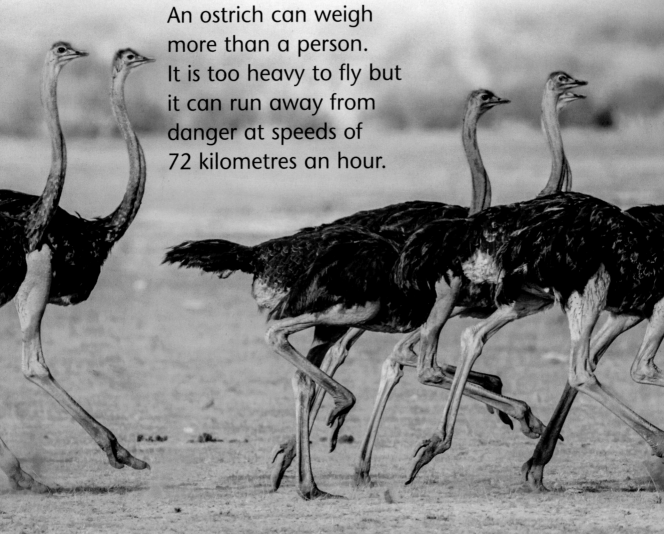

Flying underwater

Penguin wings are flat and stiff, too small for flight, but they make perfect paddles for diving and swimming underwater.

Look, no wings!

Kiwis, from New Zealand, have no natural predators and feed on the ground. So there is no need to fly and kiwis do not have wings at all!

Hardworking feathers

Birds could not fly without feathers, but feathers do other jobs too. They keep birds warm, hide them from enemies and help them communicate with their friends.

Hiding in summer

It is always hard for predators to find a ptarmigan because in summer it has dark feathers to blend in with summer plants...

Signal feathers

Macaws have brightly
coloured feathers so that
they can find each
other among the
thick leaves of
the treetops.

Hiding in winter

...but in winter the
ptarmigan stays hidden
by growing white feathers
to match the snow.

Fantastic feet

blue-footed booby

Birds' feet are made of four long toes, and covered in tough, scaly skin. Birds can do a lot more with their feet than just standing, walking or running. They use them for climbing, gripping, swimming, even for saying hello!

Feet for swimming

Many water birds have webbed feet that act as paddles for swimming. The blue-footed booby also waves its brightly coloured feet at its mate to say 'hello'.

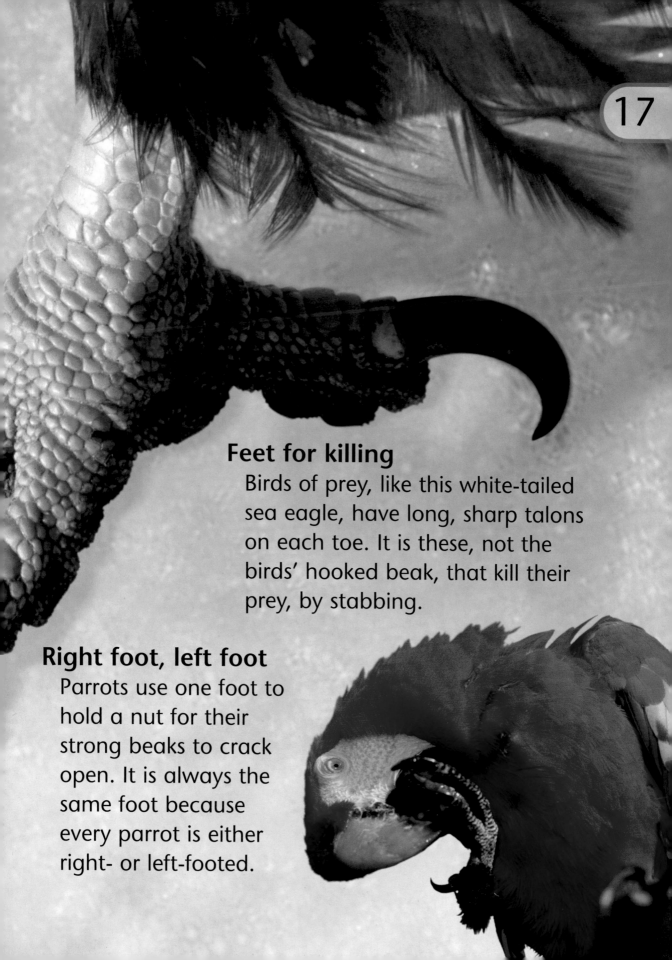

Feet for killing

Birds of prey, like this white-tailed sea eagle, have long, sharp talons on each toe. It is these, not the birds' hooked beak, that kill their prey, by stabbing.

Right foot, left foot

Parrots use one foot to hold a nut for their strong beaks to crack open. It is always the same foot because every parrot is either right- or left-footed.

Brilliant beaks

A beak is like a bird's toolkit. Every bird has a beak that gives it the right tools to help it find its food and survive!

Deep-down dinners

Curlews eat creatures like worms and snails. Their beaks can reach deep into the mud and grab prey other birds cannot get. But their delicate beaks are just as good for picking tiny creatures off the surface of the mud: two tools in one beak.

Fish hooks... and showing off!

Puffin beaks have little spines inside to hold on to slippery fish, and the bright colours send messages to other puffins.

Huge... but not heavy

A toucan's bill is long and bright, but very light because it is hollow.

Tricky tweezers

Pine cones are tough to open. Only a crossbill's beak can do the job, then pick the small, flat, juicy seeds from inside.

Super senses

Birds can use their senses – sight, hearing, touch, taste and smell – to find out about the world around them. But just like humans, their most important senses are sight and hearing.

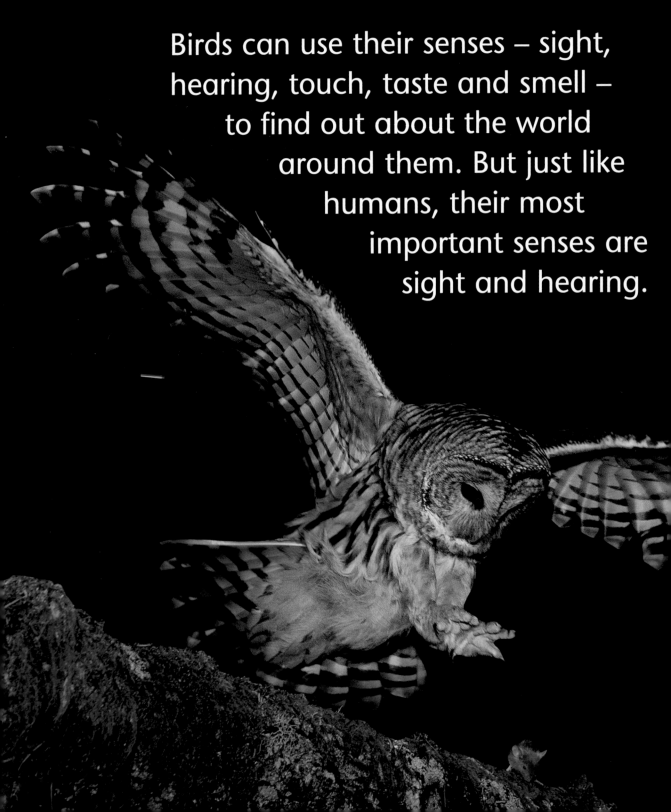

Seeing rainbows

Birds see in colour, like we do. These lorikeets eat flowers, so colour helps them to find their food among the green leaves.

I spy, with my little eye

Birds of prey, such as this kestrel, have eyes that can see three times better than humans. They can spot tiny prey on the ground while they are flying high above.

Invisible ears

Owls' ears are small holes hidden by feathers. But they are so good the owl can find a tiny mouse in the dark, just by using sound.

High-speed hunter

The peregrine falcon is the fastest and most deadly hunter on Earth. It can fly at up to 320 kilometres an hour, and its whole body is made for speed and killing.

Tools for the job

Peregrines have super-sharp eyesight for spotting prey, dagger-like talons for grabbing it, and a hooked beak for tearing flesh into bite-sized pieces.

Stooping for speed...

Peregrine wings are pointed and narrow for fast flying, but for top speeds they fold their wings and dive down in a 'stoop'.

...and for killing

Stooping is how peregrines catch almost all their prey. They stoop on flying birds, hitting them with their talons at more than 160 kilometres an hour.

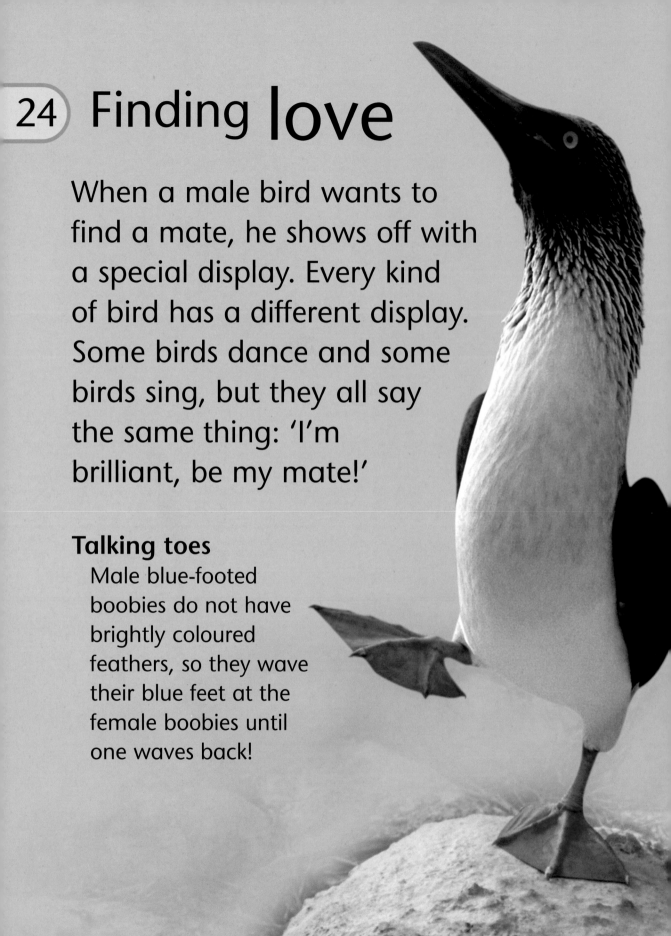

Finding love

When a male bird wants to find a mate, he shows off with a special display. Every kind of bird has a different display. Some birds dance and some birds sing, but they all say the same thing: 'I'm brilliant, be my mate!'

Talking toes

Male blue-footed boobies do not have brightly coloured feathers, so they wave their blue feet at the female boobies until one waves back!

Brilliant building

The male satin bowerbird builds a twig bower and decorates it with blue pebbles, shells and flowers so that a female will notice him. He will even use human litter, as long as it is blue!

Dancing cranes

Male and female cranes get to know each other by dancing, flapping wings and bobbing heads to the sounds of their own calls.

Making a home

Birds are fantastic builders!
They make nests of all sizes
and shapes to keep their
eggs and babies safe
from bad weather
and predators.

Stick mountain
Ospreys make their nests
by piling sticks in a tree.
The nests are too big and
heavy to blow away and too
high for any hungry
predators to reach.

Hanging around

Weaver birds use grass to weave a ball-shaped nest with one tiny entrance hole. The nest dangles from a twig, so the only way in is by flying.

Tree houses

Hoopoes like hollow trees. They are secure and cosy, and just need lining with grass and leaves to make a nest.

Life is egg-shaped!

All birds start life as an egg, laid by their mother. The baby bird grows inside, fed by the yellow yolk and protected by the hard outside shell.

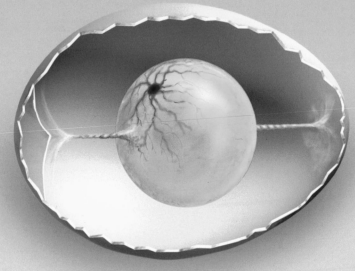

1 A warm start
Inside the egg, the chick starts to grow as soon as incubation begins. It is just a tiny blob, but changes very quickly.

2 Fast food
Food goes straight into the growing chick's tummy from the yolk, and its poo comes out into a little sac.

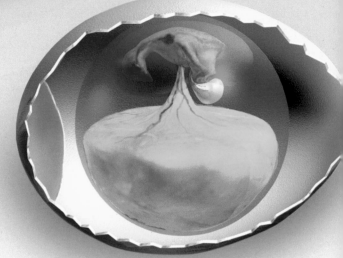

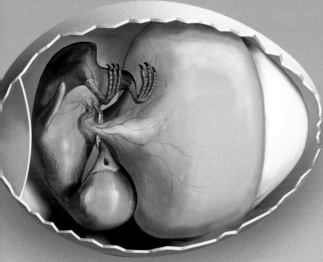

3 Getting into position

As the chick grows and uses up the yolk, it moves to the rounded end of the egg. Its eyes and beak are already formed.

4 Ready for the world

The chick is so big it fills the whole egg! When it is ready to hatch, the chick breaks the air sac and starts to breathe.

Mother hen

As soon as the chick starts breathing, it calls to its mother and she calls back. The birds learn to know each others' voices!

Feathers and fluff

Baby birds do not have proper feathers. Some are covered in fluffy down when they hatch, but others are completely naked and grow fluffy feathers later.

Helpless hatchlings

When owlets hatch, they are blind, almost naked and helpless. These have grown their first feathers.

Looking out

This baby duck's eyes are open, even before it is out of the egg!

Wet-look fluff

It is covered in downy feathers, that are still wet at first...

Ready to go

...but they soon dry. In a few hours the duckling can leave the nest and follow its mother to look for food.

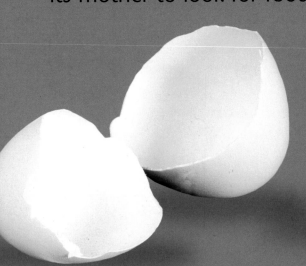

Bringing up babies

Baby birds are hard work! Bird parents have lots of different ways of giving their babies all the care and food they need.

It takes two

Both albatross parents have to search hundreds of kilometres of ocean to find enough food for their one chick.

Cheating cuckoos

Cuckoos lay eggs in other birds' nests. The baby cuckoo hatches and pushes the other eggs out. The adult birds raise the cuckoo instead of their babies.

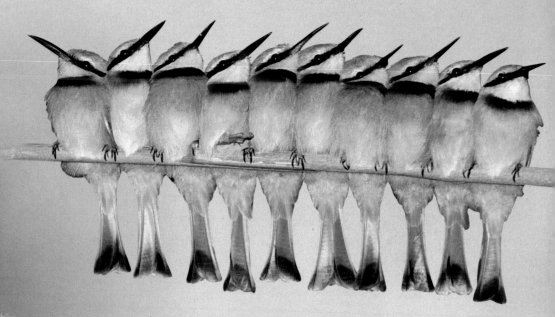

Team work

Mum, dad and a whole team of older brothers and sisters work together to feed the bee-eater babies. The more food they collect, the better chance the babies have of surviving.

Living together

On its own, a bird has just one pair of eyes to look out for danger or for food. But in a flock, there are hundreds of pairs of eyes watching too! The first flamingo to spot trouble raises the alarm and all the flock can fly away.

Party birds

Flamingoes feed and breed
together in huge flocks of
thousands of birds. They
can make whole lakes look
pink from far away.

Long-haul
travellers

Every autumn, millions of birds all over the world fly across seas, deserts and mountains to escape from winter, and to find warm weather and food. In the spring, they fly all the way back again!

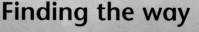

Finding the way
Geese fly in a 'V' formation. This means they can always see the bird in front, which leads the way.

Fat for flying

At migration time, birds
get fat to give them the
energy they need for
their journey.

Safety in numbers

Birds gather together before
migration, and travel in large
flocks. This means they all leave at
the right time and no one gets lost!

Birds in danger

People are bad news for birds. Hundreds of birds are in danger of becoming extinct because of what we have done. But it is not too late to make things better.

Pet parrots

Wild parrots are sometimes sold as pets. We can stop this by never buying birds that have been taken from the wild.

Bathing birds

Oil spills kill millions of seabirds. Many birds can be saved by washing them clean, and keeping them safe and warm until their feathers have dried.

Condors going up!

Rare Californian condors nearly became extinct. In 1987, there were only 22 Californian condors left in the world. Then they were bred in zoos, and put back in the wild. Now there are almost 200!

Losing their homes

The forests where the Philippine eagles live are being cut down. But local people are learning how to protect the birds and their forest homes.

The secret life of birds

There are lots of things we do not know about birds. Scientists have developed different ways of finding out more about their mysterious lives.

Penguin radio

The radio tag on this Adelie penguin's back sends out a signal that tells scientists how far it travels and how deep it dives to find its food.

Give me a ring!

The ring being put on this bird's leg carries a unique number, so the bird can be tracked all its life to find out how long it lives.

Who's who?

Coloured rings on this rare wrybill's legs help us tell it apart from other wrybills. Scientists can work out how many there are left and find ways to help protect them.

Make a bird book

Make your own bird scrapbook

It is fun to keep a scrapbook about all the different types of bird you see. You can note down what they look like, where you saw them and what time of year it was. All these things will help you to understand birds better.

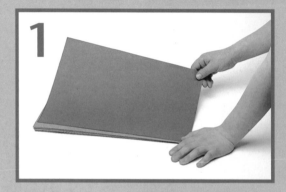

Collect some sheets of different coloured plain paper. If necessary, trim the pages so that they are all about the same size.

You will need
- Coloured paper
- Hole punch
- Ribbon or string
- Sweet wrappers
- Feathers
- Sequins
- Wrapping paper
- Orange peel
- Scissors
- Paint brush
- Glue

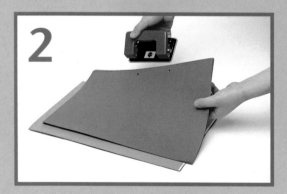

Taking care to keep your fingers out of the way, punch holes in the pages of your book. Make sure that all the holes line up.

Thread some brightly coloured ribbon or string through all the pages, to keep them together. Leave the ends at the front.

Tie the ends of the ribbon together in a loose bow. This will mean that the pages turn more easily, without ripping.

Draw a picture of a bird on the front of your book. Think about the different colours and textures of the materials you have gathered, and make a collage. The beak is hard, so card or plastic will be good. Birds' feet are scaly, so dried orange peel or sequins will give the right texture.

Collect feathers and sweet wrappers to decorate the front of your book. Dried orange peel adds texture.

Feed the birds

Make a bird table

Birds make welcome visitors to any home. Encourage local birds to dine at this easy-to-make bird table.

1

Very carefully, cut the sides out of a clean, empty ice cream carton. Leave wide 'legs' of plastic at each corner.

You will need
- Ice cream carton
- Scissors
- Modelling clay
- Compass
- String
- Bird seed

2

Using a compass, make a hole near the top and the base of each leg. Use a lump of modelling clay to protect your hands.

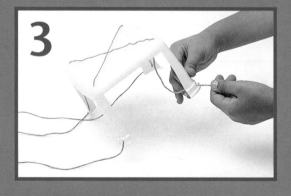

3

Thread the string through the holes, making a cross on the bottom and leaving long ends. You can tie the ends over a branch to hang your table. Put in plenty of bird seed and watch for visitors.

Seed cake treat

Every bird has its favourite food, but this bird cake is a treat many will enjoy.

You will need
- Plastic cup
- String or wire
- Scissors
- Modelling clay
- Saucepan
- Wooden spoon
- Lard or solid fat
- Bird seed

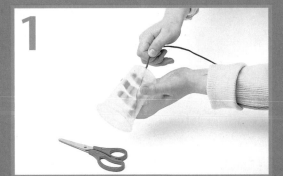

Make a hole in the bottom of a plastic cup, protecting your hands with a ball of modelling clay. Thread the string or wire through.

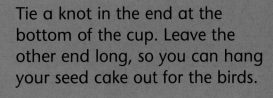

Tie a knot in the end at the bottom of the cup. Leave the other end long, so you can hang your seed cake out for the birds.

Ask an adult to melt some fat in a saucepan, then carefully stir in the seeds. Fill the cup with the mixture, keeping the string free.

Once the cake has set, carefully cut away the cup. Now you can hang the cake outside for the birds to feast on.

Using nestboxes

Different homes for different birds

Each kind of bird has its favourite place to nest. So when you put up a nestbox, make sure it is the right shape and size, and in the right place, for the birds in your area.

Ducks in trees

Black-bellied whistling ducks like to nest in holes in trees. Boxes attached to tree trunks are just as good!

Pretend it is a hole

Many small birds, such as tits, nest in tree holes. A box with a small entrance to keep out predators seems just like a treehole to a tit.

Up on the roof
Storks like to nest in high trees or on rooftops, but a special platform like this above the roof of a house is even better!

Treetop owls
Barn owls want to feel safe, high up in an old barn, or in a treehole. So this big nestbox five metres up a wall is safe and sound.

Making the birds welcome
- Choose the right box for the birds you want to attract
- Make sure it is firmly attached to a tree or wall
- Check the fittings each year and replace any damaged parts
- If you have to visit the box, do so quietly
- Do not re-visit your nestbox once a family has adopted it
- Remove old nests at the end of each season

Glossary

Air sac – the compartment in the large end of an egg that contains air

Albatross – a very large, white seabird

Bill – another word for a beak

Bird of prey – a bird, usually with a hooked beak and sharp talons, that hunts and feeds on other animals

Bower – an arch-shaped nest made from twigs

Communicate – to make other animals understand a message

Display – when male and female birds communicate with special calls and movements

Down – soft, hair-like feathers that cover young birds

Eagle – a large predator with a massive hooked beak and long, broad wings

Extinct – none left alive anywhere on Earth

Flock – a large group of birds

Gliding – flying with wings out, and without flapping

Hover – to stay in one place by beating the wings very fast

Hummingbird – a small, colourful bird that is able to hover as it feeds on the nectar from plants

Incubation – keeping an egg warm until it hatches

Mate – a bird's partner

Migration – making the same journey every year in the same season

Naked – without feathers or hair

Ocean – a large area of sea

Owl – a bird of prey with very large eyes that hunts at night

Owlet – a young owl

Perching – holding on to something with the feet

Predator – an animal that hunts and eats other animals

Prey – animals eaten by other animals

Radio tag – a device that sends out invisible signals that travel long distances

Soar – to fly or rise high in the air

Stooping – when a bird folds its wings and dives through the air

Talons – long, sharp, pointed claws

Unique – different to any other

'V' formation – when birds in flight form a pattern shaped like an arrowhead

Vulture – a large bird that feeds on the flesh of dead animals

Weave – to twist threads and grasses together

Webbed feet – feet with skin stretched between the toes

This book includes material that would be particularly useful in helping to teach children aged 7–11 elements of the English and Science curricula and some cross-curricular lessons, especially those involving Geography and Art.

Extension activities

Reading
Look through the book to find information on the different ways in which birds move on air, land and in the sea.

Writing
Choose three different birds and create a table comparing them. What do they eat and how do they look?

Write a short report on nests, showing the different types and locations. Why are they different for different birds?

Design a poster with a picture of a bird, with labelled boxes adding information about features such as feathers, claws, beaks and eyes.

This book has information about the ways in which birds are both helped and harmed by people. Prepare a balanced report showing both these effects.

Where would you go if you could fly? Write a story or poem in the first person (using 'I') about a person who has wings. Describe their feelings as they fly.

Write a poem about how a chick might feel as it grows and hatches from its egg. What would it see first outside the egg?

Speaking and listening
Make notes for a two-minute presentation about what different birds eat and how they find their food.

Science
The topic relates to the scientific themes of reproduction and growth (pp24–25, 26, 28–29, 30–31, 32–33), habitats (pp6, 9, 13, 14–15, 35, 36, 38–39) and materials (pp6, 8, 14–15, 16–17, 19, 26–27, 28). Children could

also use the information on bones and feathers (pp6–7, 8, 14–15, 30–31) to investigate how birds fly, and how they work against the forces of gravity and air resistance.

Cross-curricular links

Art: Read the information about bird colours on pages 14–15. Create a picture showing a habitat with a bird hidden in it.

Geography: Find parts of the world that have the types of habitats mentioned in the book.

Look at the information on pages 36–37 about migration. Find out the routes of some bird migration journeys and plot them on a map or an atlas.

Using the projects

Children can follow or adapt these projects at home. Here are some ideas for extending them:

Page 42: Keep a record in a daily diary of which birds you see the most and which you see less often.

Page 44: Experiment with different kinds of food and different locations for the bird table. Make a report on which were the most and least popular and try to work out why.

Page 45: Look at the information on beaks in this book and draw a beak that you think would be the best shape to eat the seed cake with. Observe the birds that visit. Was your design correct?

Pages 46–47: Can you design and make a birdbath too?

Did you know?

- There are 9,865 species of birds alive today. Of these, 1,227 species are under threat from extinction and 133 species of birds are known to have become extinct since the year 1500.

- If an animal has feathers, then it is definitely a bird. However, birds are not the only animals that can fly. Bats and flying insects have been around for millions of years.

- Some geese and ducks fly at incredible heights. Bar-headed geese have been recorded flying at almost 9,000 metres when they migrate over the Himalayas! That's nine kilometres above our heads, even higher than Mount Everest!

- The European swift never touches the ground. It eats, drinks, sleeps and even mates while flying.

- Hummingbirds are the only birds that can fly backwards. Their wings can beat up to 200 times per second when they are diving.

- Owls cannot turn their eyes. Instead, they rotate their heads up to 270 degrees, but they cannot turn their heads all the way around.

- Speeds of 320 kilometres per hour are normal during a peregrine falcon's hunting dive and a speed of 389 kilometres per hour has been recorded.

- Birds don't chew their food. They use their bills to tear food, or to crush lumpy bits before swallowing them.

Many owls have ears at different places on their heads. This gives the birds excellent hearing and helps them to find prey, even when they can't see it.

- Male weaver birds construct their nests during the mating season, to attract a mate. The female will refuse to mate with a male who has built an untidy nest.

- King and emperor penguins do not build nests. Instead, they tuck their eggs and chicks on top of their feet and under their bellies to keep them warm in the freezing winter.

The ostrich lays the world's largest egg. The egg of the hummingbird is the world's smallest.

- Most birds sit on their eggs to incubate them, but a scrub hen buries its eggs in the side of a volcano to keep them warm.

- The bird with the most feathers is the whistling swan, which can have up to 25,000 feathers during winter.

- Flying in flocks uses less energy. Geese in a V-formation may save up to 20 per cent of the energy they would need to fly alone.

- A bird's bill continues to grow throughout its life. This prevents the bill becoming too small as it wears down.

- A Manx shearwater seabird was ringed as an adult in Northern Ireland in 1953. It was retrapped 50 years later, proving that shearwaters can live for a very long time!

- Flamingo chicks are born with grey feathers. They get their pink colour because they eat brine shrimp, which contain a colouring called carotene also found in carrots.

Birds quiz

The answers to these questions can all be found by looking back through the book. See how many you get right. You can check your answers on page 56.

1) What are long, broad wings good for?
   A – Fast flapping
   B – Gliding
   C – Acrobatics

2) Which of these birds can fly?
   A – Penguin
   B – Kiwi
   C – Flamingo

3) What does an eagle use to kill its prey?
   A – Its talons
   B – Its webbed feet
   C – Its beak

4) Which bird's beak can find food in deep mud?
   A – Curlew
   B – Puffin
   C – Crossbill

5) How does the male satin bowerbird attract a mate?
   A – By changing colour
   B – By hooting like an owl
   C – By decorating a nest

6) What is it called when birds move from one region to another depending on the season?
   A – Migration
   B – Incubation
   C – Predation

7) When does a chick start calling to its mother?
   A – While it is in the egg
   B – When it hatches
   C – When it is about a week old

8) What are the fluffy feathers on a baby bird called?
   A – Middle
   B – Over
   C – Down

9) What do weaver birds use to build their nests?
   A – Cotton
   B – Grass
   C – Twigs

10) What is the fastest animal on earth?
   A – Arctic tern
   B – Kestrel
   C – Peregrine falcon

11) Does a bird's skeleton weigh…
   A – Less than all its feathers?
   B – The same as all its feathers?
   C – More than all its feathers?

12) Why do scientists put rings on birds' legs?
   A – To keep them safe from predators
   B – To track where they travel
   C – To stop people selling them in pet shops

Books to read

1000 Facts – Birds by Belinda Gallacher,
 Miles Kelly Publishing, 2007

Birds (Know How, Know Why) by Jonathan
 and Keith West, Top That! Publishing,
 2005

Birds of Prey (Kingfisher Readers),
 Kingfisher Readers, 2017

Classifying Birds (Classifying Living Things)
 by Andrew Solway, Heinemann
 Library, 2009

Eagles and Other Birds (Adapted for
 Success) by Andrew Solway,
 Heinemann Library, 2006

Falcons (Amazing Animals) by Kate Riggs,
 Creative Paperbacks, 2017

The Life Cycle of Birds (From Egg to Adult)
 by Mike Unwin, Heinemann Library,
 2004

Places to visit

Slimbridge Wildfowl and Wetlands Trust
www.wwt.org.uk/visit-us/slimbridge
The grounds at Slimbridge are home
to the largest collection of swans,
ducks, flamingoes and geese in the
world. You can see many birds that
are rare or close to extinction. Visit
the hides on the wetland, and you can
also see many wild birds. If you are
lucky, you might even spot migrating
birds landing as they finish their long
journeys across the world.

The Natural History Museum, London
www.nhm.ac.uk/tring/index.html
Take a look at the exhibits in
this amazing museum. There are
thousands upon thousands of birds,
including their skeletons, their eggs
and their nests. You can learn about
some birds which are now extinct.

The Falconry Centre, North Yorkshire
www.falconrycentre.co.uk
Experience the thrill of eagles, falcons,
hawks, vultures and owls swooping
around you at this bird of prey centre.
Learn how the birds hunt and fly and
find out where they have come from
and how they are trained. You will
even get the chance to handle a
bird of prey yourself!

Websites

www.rspb.org.uk/youth
These pages on the Royal Society for
the Protection of Birds website are full
of fun activities and facts.

www.pbs.org/lifeofbirds
Read these fascinating articles to find
out how different birds behave.

www.bbc.co.uk/nature/uk/indepth
This website has top tips for attracting
birds to your garden.

Birds quiz answers

1) B	7) A
2) C	8) C
3) A	9) B
4) A	10) C
5) C	11) A
6) A	12) B